Who Was
Marie Antoinette?

Who Was
Marie Antoinette?

by Dana Meachen Rau

illustrated by John O'Brien

Penguin Workshop

For ACR, my own queen of fashion—DMR

For Terase L. O'Brien—JO

PENGUIN WORKSHOP
An Imprint of Penguin Random House LLC, New York

Text copyright © 2015 by Dana Meachen Rau. Illustrations copyright © 2015 by John O'Brien. Cover illustration copyright © 2015 by Penguin Random House LLC. All rights reserved. Published by Penguin Workshop, an imprint of Penguin Random House LLC, New York. PENGUIN and PENGUIN WORKSHOP are trademarks of Penguin Books Ltd. WHO HQ & Design is a registered trademark of Penguin Random House LLC. Printed in the USA.

Visit us online at www.penguinrandomhouse.com.

Library of Congress Control Number: 2015953985

ISBN 9780448483108   15 14 13 12

Contents

Who Was
Marie Antoinette?

On April 21, 1770, fifteen-year-old Marie Antoinette left home and traveled to France. She had always lived a royal life. Her parents were the emperor and empress of Austria. The young archduchess was leaving behind her beloved homeland. She was engaged to marry Louis Auguste, the future king of France.

Marie Antoinette rode in a jeweled coach amid a parade of more than fifty other carriages.

Hairdressers, chefs, and other attendants traveled with her for the two-and-a-half-week journey. Peasants cheered along the road between Vienna, Austria, and Strasbourg, France. They hoped to catch a glimpse of the young bride-to-be.

The royal procession reached the Rhine River, where a new building stood on an island. Marie Antoinette said good-bye to the Austrian people who had traveled with her. When she entered the building, she had to take off all of her Austrian clothes. She was given a French gown made of golden fabric. She wasn't allowed to bring anything from Austria into France, not even Mops, her little pug dog.

In an official ceremony, she was handed over
to the French. When she opened the doors on the
side of the building that faced France, crowds of

noblemen and noblewomen greeted her. Marie Antoinette cried, but she tried to be brave.

The whole city of Strasbourg held a holiday in Marie Antoinette's honor. A French procession of carriages then carried her to her new husband and her new life at the grand palace of Versailles (ver-SIGH).

Marie Antoinette became the queen of France while still only a teenager. She had no idea how to be a good leader. Many people in France were poor. They had to pay high taxes. Their taxes went to the royal family. Some of the money was spent running the government. But plenty was also spent on gowns, jewels, parties, and fancy palaces. The common people became angry with their king and queen for wasting money while they had so little. By the end of Marie Antoinette's life, the French people were cheering for her death.

Chapter 1
The Archduchess

Emperor Francis and Empress Maria Theresa of Austria ruled over a large area of central Europe. Maria Theresa, who had inherited the throne from her father, was a strong and determined woman. On the

EMPRESS MARIA THERESA

night of November 2, 1755, she took a break from her reports and other government paperwork when her labor pains grew too strong.

In the evening, she gave birth to Maria Antonia
Josepha Joanna. Emperor Francis announced the
arrival of his daughter to the members of his royal
court gathered at their palace in Vienna.

Maria Antonia joined a household already
full of archdukes and archduchesses—four
brothers and seven sisters. Another brother would
be born the following year! It was royal tradition to
give all the archduchesses the first name "Maria."
The girls were called by their second names, so
Maria Antonia's parents called her Antonia.

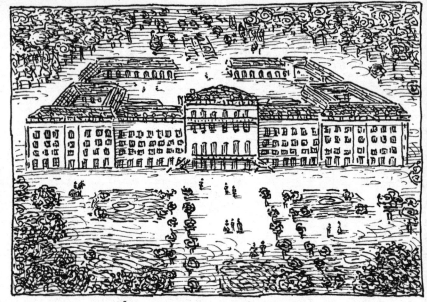

SCHÖNBRUNN PALACE

The family spent winters at their palace in
the heart of the city. In the spring and summer,
however, they moved to another enormous palace
about five miles away. Decorated with mirrors,
painted ceilings, and tapestries on the walls,
this palace had many rooms for each child. It was
surrounded by the gardens and woods of a five-
hundred-acre park. There was even a zoo with a
camel, puma, and rhinoceros.

Even though Austria had an emperor *and* an empress, Maria Theresa was the ruler. Her husband, Francis, simply assisted her. Empress Maria Theresa was much too busy to watch her children. So she hired governesses to take care of them and tutors to teach them. As royalty, the archdukes and archduchesses lived a glamorous life. For fun, they spent hours riding horses and hunting. During the cold Austrian winters, they rode swan-shaped sleds through the snow.

Antonia spent more time playing on the palace grounds than paying attention to her lessons. She had a beautiful voice and performed in family concerts, singing while her brothers and sisters played the music.

In 1762, when Antonia was six years old,

a special musician visited the royal family in Vienna. His name was Wolfgang Amadeus Mozart. Mozart was the same age as Antonia. Stories say that the little musician slipped on the well-polished floor of the palace. When Antonia helped him up, Mozart declared that he wanted to marry her.

MOZART (1756–1791)

WOLFGANG AMADEUS MOZART WAS BORN IN SALZBURG, AUSTRIA. HE SHOWED MUSICAL SKILL ON THE VIOLIN AND KEYBOARD FROM THE TIME HE WAS THREE YEARS OLD. HE STARTED WRITING HIS OWN MUSIC WHEN HE WAS ONLY FIVE.

MOZART IS ONE OF THE MOST FAMOUS CLASSICAL COMPOSERS OF ALL TIME. HE IS KNOWN FOR HIS MANY SYMPHONIES, HIS CHAMBER MUSIC, AND HIS OPERAS, SUCH AS *DON GIOVANNI* AND *THE MARRIAGE OF FIGARO*.

Antonia's father, the emperor, died in August 1765. Antonia was only nine years old. The empress, now ruling with her oldest son, Joseph, had a new focus. She was determined to arrange good marriages for her daughters. At the time, royal marriages were very important. Royal couples did not marry each other for love. They married to strengthen the bond between two countries so that the countries would support each other, especially during times of war. Maria Theresa especially wanted to marry one of her daughters to Louis Auguste, the future king of France.

Austria and France had a history of conflict. More recently, however, the two countries were at peace. Maria Theresa thought a marriage between her own family—the Habsburgs—and the French Bourbon family would strengthen the ties between them. Antonia was the best choice for marriage. She was closest in age to the dauphin.

DAUPHINS AND DAUPHINES

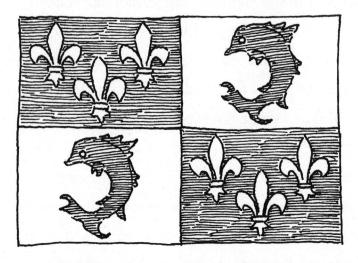

IN 1349, THE FRENCH KING PURCHASED A PIECE OF LAND CALLED THE DAUPHINÉ (THE DOLPHIN). THE LAND HAD BEEN NAMED AFTER THE DOLPHINS ON THE COAT OF ARMS OF A PREVIOUS LORD OF THE REGION, GUY IV, WHO CALLED HIMSELF THE DAUPHIN IN THE 1100S.

THE HEIR TO THOSE LANDS WAS GIVEN THE NICKNAME *DAUPHIN* (DOE-FAN). THE NAME STUCK, AND FOR THE NEXT FIVE HUNDRED YEARS *DAUPHIN* CAME TO REFER TO THE OLDEST SON OF A FRENCH KING. A DAUPHIN'S WIFE, THE FUTURE QUEEN, WAS CALLED THE *DAUPHINE* (DOE-FEEN).

The French agreed to the marriage, so the empress began to prepare her daughter. She hired a ballet teacher to help Antonia move more gracefully. A Frenchman straightened Antonia's crooked teeth with wires. A hairdresser from Paris styled her hair in the most modern ways.

France also sent a tutor, Abbé de Vermond, to the imperial palace in 1768. When Vermond met Antonia he observed, "She has a most graceful figure; holds herself well; and if . . . she grows a little taller, she will possess every good quality one could wish for in a great princess."

The thirteen-year-old archduchess was certainly charming, with her blue eyes, blond hair, and pink-and-white skin. Yet Vermond soon discovered that she knew very little. Her tutors had let her do whatever she wanted. So Vermond now made Antonia study religion, French literature, French history, and the French language.

Antonia was growing into a fine young lady, worthy to be the new French princess.

WHAT IS AN ABSOLUTE MONARCHY?

AN ABSOLUTE MONARCHY IS A FORM OF GOVERNMENT WITH A MONARCH—A KING OR QUEEN—WHO MAKES ALL THE DECISIONS FOR THE COUNTRY. MONARCHS ARE BORN TO THEIR POSITION. THIS IS KNOWN AS "INHERITING THE THRONE." THEY HOLD THE POSITIONS FOR LIFE.

LOUIS XV

IN FRANCE, ONLY MALES WERE ALLOWED TO INHERIT THE THRONE. LOUIS XV (THE FIFTEENTH) WAS THE KING OF FRANCE WHEN ANTONIA WAS BORN. HE WOULD HAVE PASSED THE TITLE OF "KING" ON TO HIS SON LOUIS FERDINAND. BUT LOUIS FERDINAND HAD DIED. SO HIS GRANDSON, LOUIS AUGUSTE, WAS NEXT IN LINE TO BECOME KING. THIS LINE OF ROYALTY IN FRANCE WAS CALLED THE BOURBON FAMILY.

IN AUSTRIA AND HUNGARY, EMPRESS MARIA THERESA HAD INHERITED THE THRONE FROM HER FATHER. HE HAD ISSUED A DECREE THAT SINCE HE HAD NO SONS, HIS DAUGHTER COULD TAKE CONTROL OF HIS EMPIRE AFTER HE DIED. THIS LINE OF ROYALTY IN AUSTRIA WAS CALLED THE HABSBURG FAMILY.

Chapter 2
A Royal Wedding

The official ceremonies for the marriage began in Vienna on April 15, 1770. The French ambassador arrived. He represented the French royal family,

who had stayed back in their palace in Versailles. Over the next few days, the Austrian imperial family held feasts and balls for their daughter. They held a ceremony to represent and celebrate the upcoming marriage, even though Louis Auguste was still in France. Antonia was now called by the French version of her name—Marie Antoinette.

On April 21, in the chilly morning, Marie Antoinette stepped into her golden carriage. Her mother said good-bye: "Farewell, my dearest child, a great distance will separate us. . . . Do so much good to the French people that they can say that I have sent them an angel."

The long procession of fifty-seven coaches journeyed across central Europe from Austria to the city of Strasbourg, France. It took more than two weeks, with about eight hours of travel each day.

Her attendants tried to make sure Marie Antoinette was comfortable. She spent her evenings in monasteries, where priests called monks lived, and also at palaces. Her hosts arranged concerts and performances. Townspeople scrambled to see her. The dauphine (future queen) was exhausted from traveling, but she had to act bright and happy for her admirers.

The procession finally arrived at the Rhine River on the border between the lands of Austria and France. Tearfully, Marie Antoinette said good-bye to her fellow travelers. She entered the Austrian side of a building specially constructed on an island in the Rhine just for the occasion. It was decorated with rugs, tapestries, and furniture borrowed from nearby wealthy families. She exited the other side to meet all of her new French attendants. Strasbourg welcomed her with ringing bells and bright fireworks. She collected the flowers that young girls threw in her path.

Another procession of carriages carried her another 250 miles to where King Louis XV and his grandson, Louis Auguste, awaited her on a quiet forest road. Marie Antoinette stepped out of her carriage and rushed up to the king. She made a deep curtsy. King Louis XV was regal and handsome. He helped her up and kissed her cheeks in welcome.

Next, Marie Antoinette faced the dauphin. Compared to the king, Louis Auguste was chubby, clumsy, and shy. They shared a small kiss. They were strangers soon to be married.

LOUIS AUGUSTE

The morning of the wedding day, May 16, 1770, Marie Antoinette arrived at the Versailles palace. She hardly had a moment to take in the splendor of her new home.

Attendants greeted her with gifts from the king—jewels, pearls, a diamond fan, and bracelets with her initials. They began the task of preparing her for her wedding. Dressing Marie

Antoinette and styling her hair took three hours.

In her white dress, Marie Antoinette joined the dauphin. He was dressed in a golden suit. They headed to the Royal Chapel. Here, they knelt at the altar and became man and wife.

THE HALL OF MIRRORS

VERSAILLES IS A HUGE PALACE OUTSIDE PARIS WITH SEVEN HUNDRED ROOMS. ONE OF THE MOST FAMOUS ROOMS IS THE HALL OF MIRRORS. THIS PASSAGEWAY IS ABOUT 240 FEET LONG AND 40 FEET HIGH, WITH 17 WINDOWS FACING THE BACK GARDENS. ON THE WALL OPPOSITE THE WINDOWS HANGS A SERIES OF MIRRORS. THE OUTDOOR LIGHT REFLECTS OFF NOT ONLY THE 357 MIRRORS

IN THE ROOM BUT ALSO THE LARGE CHANDELIERS
HANGING FROM THE CEILING.

THE HALL OF MIRRORS WAS A GATHERING
PLACE FOR THE COURT. PEOPLE GOSSIPED ABOUT
THE ACTIONS AND FASHIONS OF THE COURT. THIS
FAMOUS HALLWAY WAS THE BEST SPOT TO LEARN
NEWS OF THE ROYAL FAMILY AND THE NOBILITY.

About six thousand people had been invited to the wedding. They watched the royal family enjoy a feast in the newly built Opera House at Versailles. Food was given out in the streets, and fountains were filled with wine. Celebrations continued over the next two weeks with acrobatic shows, masked balls, and fireworks displays. All of France celebrated the marriage of the young couple.

Chapter 3
Trying to Fit In

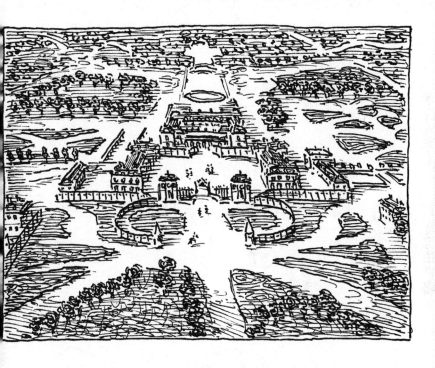

The palace at Versailles was beyond fancy. It was richly decorated with gold and marble, mirrors, and thousands of arched windows.

Paintings on the ceilings and the walls, sculptures, and tapestries adorned the rooms and hallways. The gardens were equally fancy. A large body of water, called the Grand Canal, covered just a small part of the two-thousand-acre grounds.

Throughout French history, the monarch and his family had lived in Paris, France's capital city. The city palace was called the Tuileries (TWEE-luh-ree). But Louis XIV (the Fourteenth) built a new palace in the village of Versailles, about twelve miles away. He moved there in 1682.

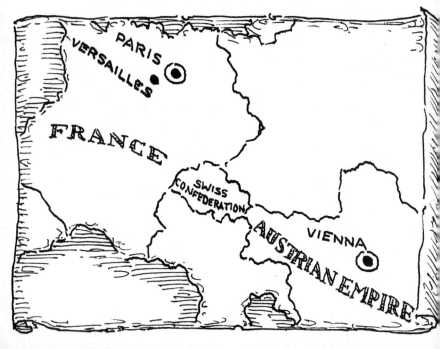

The palace was the home of the French royal family, as well as wealthy and important noble families. The palace at Versailles was also the seat of the French government. Every day, about ten thousand people walked its halls. Crowds visiting the palace could even buy souvenirs in the courtyard.

Marie Antoinette had her own rooms, including a room for guards, a room for public events, a room for her ladies-in-waiting, and a bedchamber. She was certainly used to royal life. But she was not used to being on constant display as the future queen. She had to respect the rules and customs of the French court. And there were *lots* of rules. French royalty followed guidelines about how to speak to people, how to dress, and how to eat.

Each day followed a strict schedule. Marie Antoinette woke between nine and ten. Most mornings, she ate breakfast while taking a bath,

wearing a flannel dress for modesty while in the water. Then she got dressed. This was called the *lever* (luh-VAY), which means "to get up." The *lever* was like a tourist attraction. Both men and women would come into her room to watch her get ready—not just nobles, but common people, too, as long as they were dressed nicely enough.

"I put on my rouge and wash my hands in front of the whole world," she wrote in a letter to her mother. The men would then leave, and Marie Antoinette's attendants would finish dressing her in front of her female audience.

GETTING DRESSED

MARIE ANTOINETTE OFTEN CHANGED HER CLOTHES THREE OR MORE TIMES A DAY. EACH OUTFIT HAD MANY PARTS.

FIRST, SHE PUT ON A LOOSE SLIP CALLED A *CHEMISE* (SHUH-MEEZ). THEN, A CORSET, WITH STRIPS OF WHALEBONE TO MAKE IT STIFF, WAS LACED AROUND HER RIBS AND PULLED TIGHT. ATTENDANTS TIED *PANNIERS* (PAN-EE-YAY) TO HER HIPS. THESE BASKETLIKE FORMS MADE HER SKIRT STICK OUT ON BOTH SIDES. SHE WORE HOOPSKIRTS OVER THE *PANNIERS* TO MAKE HER DRESS LOOK FULLER. A HEAVY GOWN WAS ADDED ON TOP. THEN A TRAIN WAS ATTACHED TO THE BACK OF THE GOWN. THIS WAS A LONG PIECE OF CLOTH THAT FELL FROM HER SHOULDERS ALL THE WAY TO THE FLOOR. SHE WORE SILK STOCKINGS AND SATIN HIGH-HEELED SHOES.

HER EXPENSIVE CLOTHES WERE THEN COVERED WITH A CAPE SO THE HAIRDRESSER COULD POWDER HER HAIR WITH FLOUR. THICK WHITE MAKEUP WAS APPLIED OVER HER FACE, AND TWO RED CIRCLES OF MAKEUP WERE DRAWN ONTO HER CHEEKS. THIS ELABORATE FORM OF DRESS AND DECORATION WAS MEANT TO SHOW MARIE ANTOINETTE'S WEALTH AND POWER.

When she was finished dressing, Marie Antoinette attended a Catholic Mass at the Royal Chapel. Daily Mass was followed by a public dinner in the afternoon with her husband.

Crowds looked on as if watching a show. She
visited with the dauphin or with his three aunts
(King Louis XV's sisters), and attended lessons
with her tutor, Vermond. After music lessons, and
supper at nine, it was time for the evening *coucher*
(koo-SHAY), which means "to go to bed," also
viewed by whoever wished to watch. She finally
was tucked into her covers at 11:00 p.m.

Marie Antoinette had trouble fitting into this very public lifestyle. And even though her life was on display, she was often lonely. Her dog, Mops, had been sent to her in Versailles. But even the dog was little comfort. Her husband's old aunts were critical and harsh.

Her attendants corrected and nagged her. Everyone watched her closely to see if she made a mistake. She got scolded if she broke the rules. Also, some members of the court didn't like Marie Antoinette because she was Austrian.

In addition to all the new rules, Marie Antoinette had to get used to her new husband. Even though she and Louis Auguste were close in age, they were opposites. She was fun and carefree. She loved to be around people and attend parties. He was large and clumsy. He was shy and often sad. He preferred spending time alone, hunting, or studying books.

Marie Antoinette's mother lived far away, but she was aware of everything that happened in her daughter's life. The Austrian ambassador to France, Count Mercy, and Vermond acted as her spies. Marie Antoinette would confide in them, and they would report all the details back to the empress. In regular letters, the empress scolded her daughter. She wished Marie Antoinette

COUNT MERCY

would pay more attention to her husband and spend less time at parties. Marie Antoinette felt pressure from her mother. "I love the Empress," she wrote, "but I'm frightened of her, even at a distance."

In June 1773, Marie Antoinette started to feel more at home in France. After three years of marriage, she was presented to the people of Paris.

She made an official entrance into the capital city. The Parisians welcomed Louis Auguste and Marie Antoinette with trumpets, cannons, and cheers. The governor gave them the keys to the city.

Marie Antoinette was glad that the public seemed to like her. She was most pleased with "the tenderness and eagerness of the poor people, who, in spite of the taxes which oppress them, were carried away with joy on seeing us." The common people hoped for a brighter future. They hoped for an end to their poverty when Louis Auguste and Marie Antoinette became king and queen.

Chapter 4
Living Like a Queen

In the spring of 1774, King Louis XV became ill. He felt feverish and broke out into a rash. He had smallpox. At the time, there was no cure for this disease. In less than two weeks the king was dead.

King Louis XV's death meant it was time for
Louis Auguste to step up to his new position. He
was crowned the king of France at a ceremony
on June 11, 1775. Marie Antoinette was proud as
she looked on. "I couldn't contain my emotion;"

she wrote, "tears rolled down my face in spite of myself and people took kindly to it." Louis Auguste became Louis XVI (the Sixteenth). He was only twenty—and Marie Antoinette was only nineteen—when they became king and queen.

The king's ministers were worried that Louis was not prepared to rule. They didn't know what to expect from the queen.

According to French laws, queens didn't have any power. Marie Antoinette's job was to set a good example for the French people. She was to be graceful and kind, obey her husband, and have children. But Marie Antoinette's mother, Empress Maria Theresa, wanted her daughter to keep the ties between Austria and France strong. The empress insisted on knowing everything that went on at Versailles. She wanted her daughter to have influence over the king. She wanted Marie Antoinette to help make political decisions.

Marie Antoinette, however, wanted to live the way *she* wanted. She was not interested in following the customs of other French queens. And she was tired of listening to her mother. As queen, she could now do whatever she wanted. And she wanted to enjoy herself.

It was easy to be spoiled at Versailles. Her household (all the people who attended to her) totaled about five hundred people! She had ladies to help her dress, people to serve her food, and men to take care of her horses. She even had a trainbearer whose job was to hold the back of her gown off the floor when she walked.

France was known as the fashion center of the world, and Marie Antoinette set the fashion trends.

Mademoiselle Rose Bertin was her personal dressmaker. She came to the queen's chambers about twice a week. She made dresses with tight tops and wide skirts out of satin, velvet, and rich brocade fabric. They were decorated with jewels,

pearls, ribbons, and lace. The queen's wardrobe filled three entire rooms!

The young queen also invited the royal jewelers to show her their latest creations. She especially liked to buy diamonds of all sorts—set in rings, as necklaces, or as earrings. One set of her diamond earrings dangled like the palace chandeliers.

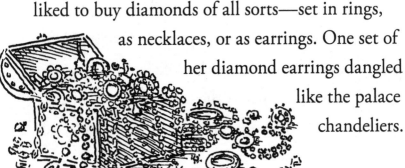

Her personal hairdresser, Léonard Autié, also came to the palace. French noble people commonly wore wigs. It was a sign of their high position, but Marie Antoinette took wigs to new heights. The most famous hairstyle was called the pouf.

Besides being fashionable, poufs also told stories. Some held scenes of nature, with tiny figures of farmers or animals. Some had moving parts, like flapping birds. After a French victory at sea against the British, Marie Antoinette wore a model of a ship in her hair. She also decorated her head as a vegetable garden, complete with radishes, carrots, and a head of cabbage. No matter how silly the poufs seemed, everyone copied the queen's hairstyle.

THE POUF

THE POUF WAS A VERY DELICATE HAIRSTYLE THAT TOOK HOURS TO CREATE. THE MINUTE MARIE ANTOINETTE HEARD OF IT, SHE WANTED TO WEAR IT. A METAL FRAME WAS SET UPON THE HEAD TO GIVE STRUCTURE TO THE SHAPE OF THE HAIR. IT WAS THEN PADDED WITH BOTH FAKE HAIR AND THE REAL HAIR OF THE WEARER. ONCE THE SHAPE WAS CREATED, THE POUF WAS FINISHED WITH WHITE OR GREY POWDER. 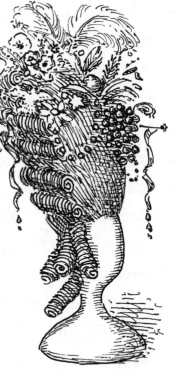 DECORATIONS OF ALL SORTS, SUCH AS FLOWERS, FEATHERS, FRUIT, BIRDS, AND RIBBONS COMPLETED THE STYLE. POUFS COULD BE SMALL. BUT MARIE ANTOINETTE'S POUFS SOMETIMES TOWERED THREE FEET ABOVE HER HEAD!

A POUF WOULD LAST FOR ABOUT A WEEK, OR UNTIL IT LOST ITS SHAPE.

Poufs may have been stylish at the time, but they were not sensible or comfortable. The cage of hair was quite heavy. At the theater, poufs blocked the viewers sitting behind them. In carriages, ladies might have to sit on the floor instead of the coach's seat because their poufs hit the ceiling. Sleeping was difficult—poufs had to be wrapped up like a package, and the wearer might even have to sleep sitting up. The warm dark space on a woman's head under a pouf was the perfect place for bugs and lice to live. Some ladies used long-armed tools to reach under the wigs and scratch their itchy scalps.

Marie Antoinette surrounded herself with young people and had a close circle of favorites.

The king often went to bed early, but Marie Antoinette and her friends gambled all night or rushed off to late-night parties in Paris. Every Monday evening, she treated guests to masked balls. She held hunting parties and played billiards and cards.

While Marie Antoinette giggled, flirted, and made up her own rules, she offended many important noble families. French royalty had always lived a fancy lifestyle, but the court felt that Marie Antoinette wasn't serious enough about being a queen. But Marie Antoinette did not change her ways. Instead the young queen found a place to escape from these critical eyes. A smaller, quiet house, called Petit Trianon (puh-TEE TREE-uh-nawhn), was a gift from her husband in 1775.

Besides the noble families at court, many French people were beginning to dislike the new queen. They spread gossip and rumors about her. They made fun of her clothes and hair. They scoffed at the money she spent. A song could be heard around court:

You've given offense a-plenty
Little queen of only twenty

You'll go home to Austria
Fa-lal-lal, fal-lal . . .

Marie Antoinette continued to do what she wished. After all, she was the queen!

PETIT TRIANON

PETIT TRIANON WAS A HOUSE IN THE CORNER OF THE PALACE GROUNDS. IT HAD ONLY SEVEN ROOMS. UNLIKE THE VERY PUBLIC SPACES IN VERSAILLES, PETIT TRIANON WAS JUST FOR MARIE ANTOINETTE AND HER PERSONAL GUESTS. EVEN THE KING HAD TO BE INVITED. SHE REDECORATED THE ROOMS, REDESIGNED THE GARDENS, AND HELD PARTIES AND PLAYS.

Chapter 5
Motherhood

Everyone in France was waiting for Marie Antoinette to become a mother. The royal Bourbon line needed a son to take over the throne after the king died. Not only were the French people angry at her for not having a baby, but her mother was, too. The empress continued to send Marie Antoinette scolding letters. She even sent her son, Emperor Joseph, to talk some sense into her daughter.

Joseph came to Versailles in April 1777 and stayed for six weeks. While there, he lectured his sister about her foolish friends, silly hair and makeup, and wasteful gambling.

To everyone's relief, Marie Antoinette finally became pregnant. On December 20, 1778, the king, the royal family, and a crowd of guests filled her bedchamber. The crowd watched the twenty-three-year-old queen give birth to a baby girl—

not an heir to the throne. Many people were disappointed. But Marie Antoinette told her baby daughter, Maria Therese, whom they called Madame Royale: "Poor little girl, you are not what was desired, but you are no less dear to me on that account. A son would have been the property of the state. You shall be mine."

Around the time of Madame Royale's birth, the king and the French government were focused on America. The colonies there had declared independence from England. They no longer wanted to be ruled by a king, and they fought against England in the American Revolution. King Louis XVI sided with the Americans. This led to England declaring war on France. Many French noblemen left to fight in America. With so much attention and money devoted to war, however, little was left for the poor people of France.

Marie Antoinette didn't concern herself with politics, especially now that she was a mother. She tried to live a more private life, spending lots of time at Petit Trianon. The queen dressed more simply, wearing gowns of plain white fabric tied with a sash. She wore her hair loose and topped it with a straw hat.

She created a tiny farm community on the grounds of Petit Trianon. There was a farmhouse, a barn, a henhouse, a mill, and cottages, as well as cows, sheep, goats, and poultry. It was created to look as if it had been there for many years. She hired a farmer, gardeners, and cattlemen to take care of the fields and animals.

Marie Antoinette and her friends enjoyed living what they considered to be a simple life in her pretend village. At the same time, common people in *real* villages around France suffered and starved.

Rumors and gossip spread as Marie Antoinette spent so much time away from the palace.

Nobles were jealous that they weren't invited
to Petit Trianon. People were angry that she no
longer wore dresses made of French silk. She
was the French queen, after all! Most of all, even
though royal families had done so for centuries,
they were upset that Marie Antoinette spent so
much money that they felt belonged to France and
its people!

But the people of France had
new faith in their queen after
she had another baby
on October 22, 1781.
It was a boy! Sadly,
Marie Antoinette's
mother, Empress Maria
Theresa of Austria,
had died in late 1780.
She did not live to see
her daughter finally
give birth to a son.

LOUIS JOSEPH

The king and queen named him Louis Joseph. The king said to his wife, "Madame, you have fulfilled our wishes and those of France—you are the mother of a dauphin." All of France celebrated.

The Bourbon line was further ensured when Marie Antoinette gave birth to another son, Louis Charles, on March 27, 1785. Finally, Marie Antoinette had fulfilled her duty as queen not just once, but twice. But the support of the people wouldn't last long.

A FASHIONABLE COLOR

THE WHOLE COUNTRY REJOICED WHEN MARIE ANTOINETTE GAVE BIRTH TO THE DAUPHIN, LOUIS JOSEPH. GIFTS POURED IN FROM NOT ONLY NOBLE FAMILIES BUT ALSO THE BUTCHERS, BAKERS, SHOEMAKERS, LOCKSMITHS, AND ALL THE PEOPLE OF THE TOWN OF VERSAILLES. THE ARRIVAL OF LOUIS JOSEPH EVEN CREATED A TREND IN THE FASHION WORLD. A NEW BROWNISH-GREEN FABRIC COLOR BECAME POPULAR. IT WAS CALLED *CACA-DAUPHIN*, WHICH MEANS "THE DAUPHIN'S POOP."

Chapter 6
Scandal and Suffering

Even though Marie Antoinette enjoyed motherhood, the people of France continued to find reasons to dislike her. The summer of 1785 brought a huge scandal. It became known as the Diamond Necklace Affair.

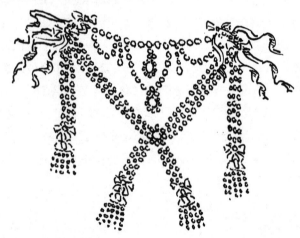

A jeweler for the royal family asked the queen to pay him for a large and expensive diamond necklace. Marie Antoinette had no idea what he was talking about. The jeweler said that he had given the necklace to Cardinal Louis de Rohan, a church official, to present to the queen.

CARDINAL LOUIS DE ROHAN

Marie Antoinette had never asked for the necklace. She knew nothing about it and was convinced that Cardinal Rohan was trying to make her look bad. She had King Louis arrest him. During the trial, the real story came out. A lady of the court had forged a note from the queen, asking Rohan for the necklace. When Rohan gave it to the lady, instead of handing it over to the queen, she gave it to her husband.

He, in turn, brought it to London and sold the diamonds. Cardinal Rohan was found to be innocent.

Marie Antoinette was not happy with the verdict. She still wanted Rohan punished. So Louis sent him away from court. This angered noble families that had supported the cardinal. Even though Marie Antoinette had never asked for the necklace in the first place, she was still seen as guilty in the eyes of the people. She had sent an innocent man away.

Life continued to go badly for the queen. In July 1786, she gave birth to a baby girl who died the following summer. And Marie Antoinette's oldest boy, Louis Joseph, was very ill.

The government of France wasn't doing well, either. The high costs of supporting the American Revolution along with the king and queen's spending left the country with no money. The people of France were furious. They placed a lot of the blame on Marie Antoinette. Rumors spread about her in pamphlets and flyers. Crude cartoons made fun of her and blamed her for all the country's problems. People hissed at her in public. She discovered threats to her life on signs near her seats at the theater.

Les deux ne font qu'un

"LET THEM EAT CAKE!"

HERE IS ONE OF MANY RUMORS SPREAD ABOUT MARIE ANTOINETTE. THE STORY WAS SAID TO REVEAL MARIE ANTOINETTE'S CLUELESS ATTITUDE TOWARD THE PEASANTS. WHEN TOLD THAT THE STARVING PEOPLE NEEDED BREAD, SHE REPLIED, "LET THEM EAT CAKE!" THE REMARK WAS MEANT TO SHOW HOW OUT OF TOUCH SHE WAS WITH THE PROBLEMS OF THE POOR.

BUT THIS STORY WAS NOT TRUE. SIMILAR WORDS WERE ACTUALLY SAID BY THE WIFE OF LOUIS XIV (THE FOURTEENTH)—TWO KINGS BEFORE LOUIS XVI—ABOUT ONE HUNDRED YEARS EARLIER.

To make matters worse, the summer of 1788 brought terrible weather that resulted in a poor harvest. Bread prices rose throughout the country because there wasn't enough wheat. The rough summer was followed by an especially cold winter. The poor people of France were starving and dying. They started to question their government. They wondered how the king, queen, and nobility could continue to have such fancy parties and eat such expensive food.

Spring finally arrived, but it didn't bring much relief. The sickly Louis Joseph died on June 4, 1789. His younger brother, Louis Charles, was now the dauphin.

King Louis XVI was under pressure to do something for the French people. He called a meeting of the Estates General in May 1789. This group represented the three parts of French society— nobility, clergy (priests, bishops, and cardinals), and common people. The common people were known as the Third Estate. The Estates General couldn't agree on how to fix France's problems.

Each order had one vote, which was unfair to the Third Estate, which represented the most people.

The Third Estate was fed up. Inspired by the American Revolution, the common people rose up and started a revolution. They broke away from the Estates General to form a new group—the National Assembly. They gave themselves the power to make laws. This was not what Louis XVI and Marie Antoinette wanted. They hoped to protect the monarchy and the power of the king. King Louis let the National Assembly meet, but he also built up troops against them.

Fear and panic spread in the streets of Paris. On July 14, 1789, a mob gathered against the troops of the nobility. They charged on the Bastille (bah-STEE-yuh) prison, gathering ammunition, freeing prisoners, and leaving many dead and wounded behind. Soon, the revolt spread beyond Paris. Peasants were attacking nobility across the country.

The National Assembly started to write out the
Declaration of the Rights of Man and of the Citizen.
The document was like America's Declaration of
Independence. It gave the same rights to everyone,

no matter their social class. It was to be the
beginning of a constitution—a set of laws—for
a new government that would better represent
the people.

Relations between the royal family at Versailles and the people of Paris grew tense. The king and queen feared for their safety. The Parisians suspected the royals were plotting against them to protect the monarchy at all costs.

On the morning of October 5, 1789, the market women, servants, and washerwomen of Paris,

who were worried about their starving children, gathered to march through the fog and pouring rain to Versailles. National Guard troops came along to help keep order. The mob of about six thousand carried weapons, such as pitchforks, broomsticks, and some guns.

When the women arrived at the palace, muddy and tired from the walk, they demanded food from the king. A small group was invited into the palace, and Louis assured them he would provide food for the poor of Paris. But the mob outside grew more threatening. Louis and Marie Antoinette couldn't decide what to do. There was no way to escape past the crowd. Assured they would be safe, the royal family went to bed. But at about four in the morning, a few women snuck up the staircase toward the queen's rooms, killing two of her bodyguards.

King Louis walked out onto the balcony
to try to calm the crowd in the courtyard, but
they demanded to see the queen. Bravely, Marie
Antoinette stood alone before the howling mob.
She made a deep curtsy to show them respect.

The crowd shouted, "To Paris! To Paris!" They wanted the king and queen to move into the city to end the separation between the royals in their grand palace and the people they ruled over. The crowd escorted the royal family in a long procession of carriages, carrying the heads of the dead bodyguards on tall spikes.

Louis XVI, Marie Antoinette, Madame Royale, and the little dauphin left their beautiful palace forever.

Chapter 7
A Failed Escape

The king, queen, royal family, attendants, and court moved into their residence in Paris—the palace of the Tuileries. Louis and Marie Antoinette continued their customs, such as the morning *lever*, the evening *coucher*, and daily Mass. The public still came to view them, just as they had at Versailles.

In the city, the Assembly discussed creating a constitutional monarchy. In this new type of government, the king would share power with elected officials. The people would get to vote for representatives. Marie Antoinette was saddened as her husband slowly lost his control over France. Louis became sick and depressed as he gave in to the demands of the people.

Although the king and queen were living in a palace and being treated as royals, they feared this would not last much longer. So many people spoke against them that they worried for their lives. The queen told her old friend Count Mercy, "Our situation here is frightful." They decided to escape. It would be dangerous. They would have to disguise themselves and sneak out during the night.

THE PALACE OF THE TUILERIES

MONARCHS MOVED IN AND OUT OF THE PALACE OF THE TUILERIES FROM THE TIME CONSTRUCTION BEGAN IN THE 1560S. WHEN IT WASN'T HOME TO THE ROYAL FAMILY, THE TUILERIES WAS USED AS APARTMENTS FOR ARTISTS AND A PLACE FOR PERFORMANCES. EARLY IN HER REIGN, MARIE ANTOINETTE STAYED IN ONE OF ITS APARTMENTS AFTER EVENING EVENTS IN PARIS.

THE PALACE BURNED DOWN IN 1871, BUT THE GARDENS REMAIN AND ARE STILL POPULAR WITH TOURISTS TO THIS DAY.

On Monday, June 20, 1791, the king and queen acted as if it were any other day. In the evening, Marie Antoinette and the children's governess brought twelve-year-old Madame Royale and six-year-old Louis Charles to a waiting carriage. The queen finished her supper so no one would be suspicious. Madame Elisabeth, the king's sister, joined the children in the carriage. Then, as soon as their attendants left, the king and queen changed into servants' clothes and sneaked out of the palace, too.

Outside Paris, they switched to a larger carriage. It held everything that was needed for a long journey, including food and a small cookstove. The governess pretended to be a Russian aristocrat, and the royal family pretended to be her servants. They headed to a town near the French border, where they hoped to find people supportive of the king.

The carriage moved very slowly. It had to stop every fifteen miles to change horses. But the family was confident about their escape. No one seemed to be following them. In a small village, however, someone recognized them. News spread ahead to the next village. When the royal family arrived to change horses, the villagers held the family there.

Officials from the National Assembly arrived the next morning and made the carriage turn around.

The trip back to Paris was horrible—hot and slow, with mobs shouting insults at them. The journey out had taken only about one day. The trip back took four. When they returned to the palace, the king and queen were under constant watch.

On September 14, 1791, the king officially accepted the constitution drawn up by the new government. It established a Legislative Assembly of elected officials and greatly limited the king's powers. That day, Louis XVI cried.

Marie Antoinette was not ready to give up being queen. Over the winter, she devoted her energy to writing letters to other royal families in Europe. She wrote in code or invisible ink. She smuggled the letters out of the Tuileries palace inside hats or boxes of chocolate. She wrote to her brother Leopold in Austria. She wrote to the leaders of Prussia, Spain, Sweden, and Russia.

Soon, Austria and Prussia went to war against France. They wanted to restore the French king's power and remove the Legislative Assembly.

The French people, however, were determined to end the king's reign. On August 10, 1792, a mob attacked the Tuileries palace. They ripped apart the royal family's rooms, and killed their servants and guards. They took Marie Antoinette's

jewels and dragged dresses from her closets. The
royals' possessions were tossed into the streets of
Paris.

The members of the royal family had been
hiding in a safe place inside the Assembly
building. Now, however, they were political
prisoners. The large Temple Tower prison would
be their home.

Chapter 8
End of the Monarchy

Life in the prison tower was very different from what the royal family had always known. The tower had a bedroom on the second floor for the king and his son, and bedrooms and a bathroom on the third floor for Marie Antoinette, Madame Royale, and Madame Elisabeth. They all ate breakfast together.

Louis and Marie Antoinette taught their children lessons. They got fresh air on the lawn and read or sewed at night. Even though they were prisoners, servants still treated them as royals.

Meanwhile, a newly formed National Convention declared France a republic. Leaders were to be elected by the people. There was no place for a king and queen in this type of government. The king was stripped of all power.

The king was put on trial for treason, or working against the interests of his country.

The court sentenced him to death by guillotine (GEE-yoh-teen). On the evening of January 20, 1793, the king said good-bye to his family. He promised he would see them in the morning one last time, but he never did. Marie Antoinette heard drumrolls and the cheers of the French people from the tower window. She knew Louis had been killed.

THE GUILLOTINE

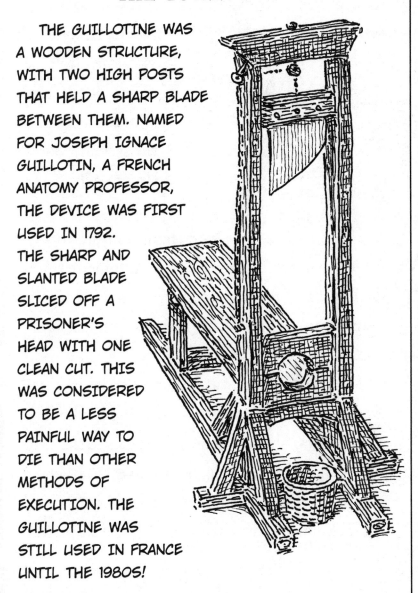

THE GUILLOTINE WAS A WOODEN STRUCTURE, WITH TWO HIGH POSTS THAT HELD A SHARP BLADE BETWEEN THEM. NAMED FOR JOSEPH IGNACE GUILLOTIN, A FRENCH ANATOMY PROFESSOR, THE DEVICE WAS FIRST USED IN 1792. THE SHARP AND SLANTED BLADE SLICED OFF A PRISONER'S HEAD WITH ONE CLEAN CUT. THIS WAS CONSIDERED TO BE A LESS PAINFUL WAY TO DIE THAN OTHER METHODS OF EXECUTION. THE GUILLOTINE WAS STILL USED IN FRANCE UNTIL THE 1980S!

That July, officials took Marie Antoinette's son away from her. They locked Louis Charles alone in the second-floor bedroom, where a cruel new tutor was in charge of him. In August, officials removed Marie Antoinette from the tower and took her to a new prison. Two soldiers sat with her in her small cell on constant watch.

Marie Antoinette was brought to trial in October 1793, four years after leaving her home in Versailles. She had changed a lot since she had been crowned queen eighteen years earlier. Her patched dress, frail body, and white hair made her look much older than her thirty-seven years.

She was accused of many crimes. Witnesses claimed that she had been plotting against France from the moment she arrived from Austria. They accused her of spying. They accused her of sending gold to her brother, the emperor of Austria. They blamed her for the king's poor decisions and mocked her extravagant lifestyle.

No one had any proof of these crimes. But everyone was looking for someone to blame for all of the problems of France. Killing the king had not been enough. Marie Antoinette was sentenced to death as well. Like Louis, her head would be cut off in public by guillotine.

In the early morning after her trial, Marie Antoinette asked her jailers for ink, a pen, and 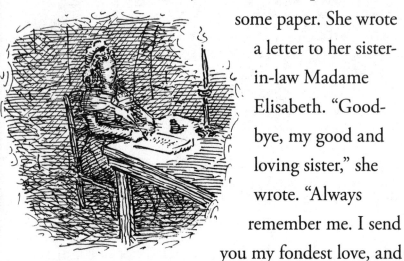 some paper. She wrote a letter to her sister-in-law Madame Elisabeth. "Good-bye, my good and loving sister," she wrote. "Always remember me. I send you my fondest love, and send it as well to my poor dear children. My God, it is agony to leave them. Good-bye. Good-bye."

The letter was never delivered.

The morning of October 16, 1793, Marie Antoinette was praying when the executioner came to collect her. He tied her hands behind her back and cut her hair short. He led her by a rope, like an animal, to an open cart. The cart, surrounded by soldiers on horses and on foot, brought her along muddy streets and through the shouting crowds. The square was already packed with people waiting to watch her die.

Marie Antoinette got out of the cart without any help, and stepped up to the scaffold. The executioner locked her into the guillotine and let the blade fall. Her head tumbled into a basket. When he lifted the head up high, the crowd yelled, "Long live the republic!" Marie Antoinette's body and head were tossed in a wheelbarrow and carted away.

The death of the king and queen did not end the French Revolution. Members of the new government disagreed. From 1793 to 1794, the government executed thousands of people by guillotine, including Madame Elisabeth. This bloody year became known as the Reign of Terror. The revolution finally ended when Napoleon Bonaparte took control of the republic in 1799. He was a strong military leader who organized France's laws,

NAPOLEON BONAPARTE

conquered other European lands, and was eventually crowned emperor of France.

The dauphin remained in the tower and died in June 1794. He was nine years old. The only one to survive was Madame Royale, the princess Maria Therese. She was released on her seventeenth birthday to the safety of Austria, where her mother's tragic story had first begun.

TIMELINE OF
MARIE ANTOINETTE'S LIFE

1755 — Maria Antonia Josepha Joanna is born on November 2 in Vienna to Maria Theresa of Austria and Francis I, Holy Roman Emperor

1770 — Leaves Austria for France on April 21
On May 16, marries Louis Auguste, the future king of France

1774 — King Louis XV dies of smallpox on May 10

1775 — Louis Auguste is crowned King Louis XVI, and Marie Antoinette becomes queen, on June 11
In August, Louis gives Petit Trianon to Marie Antoinette

1777 — Marie Antoinette's brother, Emperor Joseph of Austria, visits her at Versailles

1778 — Daughter Madame Royale is born

1780 — Mother, Empress Maria Theresa, dies

1781 — Son Louis Joseph is born

1785 — Second son, Louis Charles, is born
The Diamond Necklace Affair causes a scandal

1786 — Daughter Sophie Beatrice is born and dies less than a year later

1789 — Louis XVI calls a meeting of the Estates General in May
Marie Antoinette's son Louis Joseph dies in June
On July 14, a mob storms the Bastille prison
On October 5, the poor women of Paris march on Versailles, and the royal family is taken to Paris

1791 — In June, the royal family attempts to escape from the Tuileries

1792 — In August, the royal family is imprisoned in the Temple Tower

1793 — The king is sentenced to death and beheaded by guillotine on January 21
Marie Antoinette suffers the same fate on October 16

TIMELINE OF THE WORLD

American Benjamin Franklin experiments with electricity by flying a kite in a thunderstorm —— 1752

Britain and France fight over territories in America in the French and Indian War —— 1754–1763

A comet appears, just as English astronomer Edmond Halley (1656–1742) predicted it would, and it becomes known as Halley's Comet —— 1758

English mapmaker John Spilsbury invents the first jigsaw puzzle, showing a map of England and Wales, which is used to teach children geography —— 1767

British explorer James Cook heads out in the *Endeavor* on the first of three important expeditions in the Pacific Ocean —— 1768

James Watt creates a steam engine that uses less fuel than earlier models —— 1769

The colonies of America fight against England for independence in the American Revolution —— 1775–1783

The Montgolfier brothers, French papermakers, invent the first hot-air balloon —— 1782

Noah Webster publishes the first part of his spelling book, which will go on to sell more than seventy million copies —— 1783

Englishman Edmund Cartwright invents the first steam-powered loom for weaving thread into fabric —— 1785

The French Revolution transforms the government of France from a monarchy to a republic —— 1789–1799

Wolfgang Amadeus Mozart's opera *The Magic Flute* is performed in Vienna —— 1791

Edward Jenner, a British doctor, experiments with the first smallpox vaccination —— 1796

BIBLIOGRAPHY

Fraser, Antonia. **Marie Antoinette: The Journey**. New York: Doubleday, 2001.

Lever, Evelyne. **Marie Antoinette: The Last Queen of France**. New York: Farrar, Straus and Giroux, 2000.

"Marie Antoinette and the French Revolution." PBS.org. http://www.pbs.org/marieantoinette/ (accessed May 1, 2014).

Seward, Desmond. **Marie Antoinette**. New York: St. Martin's Press, 1981.

Weber, Caroline. **Queen of Fashion: What Marie Antoinette Wore to the Revolution**. New York: Henry Holt and Company, 2006.